index

2. Foreword

3. I reflect

4. Autism

5. Peace

6. My mind

7. Her Grace

8. Metronome of art

9. Wounded

10. Natures gift

11. Strength

12. The rain

13. Spring

14. Time in nature

15. My mind is struggle

16. Life is a game

17. Rise up

18. My thoughts

19. My Anger

20. My love

21. I need

22. Happy birthday ma

23. Dovahkiin

Foreword

My mental difficulties include schizophrenia and autism.

My search for a mental balance has been difficult and long.

I found a passion for writing poetry in a way that reflects my emotion

And it has given me the confidence to pursue my writing ability.

I want to share my experience with others in hope of one day someone

will be inspired enough to pursue their own talent.

My goal is to shed light on mental illness and show the world

That mental health can affect all of us some in less or worse ways.

So my advice is tell someone how you feel

Be more understanding when someone is low

Be the person to say i need help

We can help each other is more ways than once thought

Special thanks to family and friends who have supported me

It's because of you that I can share my voice.

i reflect

I hope for the future but regret the past
I see whos first but finnish last
The sun will rise but shadows cast
I walk alone the darkness vast
 My feeling hurt my mind harassed
I think about what have i become
An empty soul but mostly numb
My thought go wild and often run
I stand here blank i am undone
I sit alone a dangerous mind
I walked with the crowd but got left behind
The light are dimmed and never shined
Someone to love i have yet to find
I hope for help but never ask
Seeing the bright side is an endless task
I say it's hopeless but i'm afraid to die
I say it's fine but clearly lie
I am but a shadow in a stranger's eye

AUTISM

Appreciate those who have helped you

Understand those who are beside you

Think positive and focus on your goals

Is it just me? No you're not alone

See past the maze and walk the great road

Making yourself better is all that we know

Peace

Peace love pride respect

Pain sorrow abuse neglect

All have cause and effect

So treat people nice and don't forget

People have opinions so don't correct

So when you see a bunch of people

Just remember that we are all equal

Life is short the is no sequel

My mind

I try my best to reap what i sow

But time goes by and often slow

My mood swings high My emotions low

Sometimes i feel i am alone

On the cusp of madness

On the verge of insane

I walk along this existential plain

A doubtful mind in a reality of pain

I fly with clouds shadows with rain

As i walk the abyss The darkness vast

It's time for the future but i remember the past

I feel happy with memories but feelings don't last

I feel very fragile and can disappear fast

Her Grace

Her name was grace

Her eyes were peace

Her love was was forever

But never for lease

She could ride the storm

And calm the beast

Her presence was warm

Anguish decreased

I glanced at her She met my stare

Time stood still

A moment to share

If it's one thing she knows

i'll always be here

Metronome of art

The clock is ticking like a metronome of art

Feelings waver of a dying poets heart

Locked in tandem with a new life's start

And it all bellows down to a great artist mark

Time is flowing like tides adrift

Overtaken by new dawns gift

With new dawns faces spirits begin to lift

And the morning air i begin to miss

Thought spill into a long slumbers dream

And lost echos in the abyss begin to scream

And spread apart like hot waters steam

And come back together like a tailors seem

Old wars steel begins to rust

As the leaves die and turn to dust

But its natures way replacement is a must

As the bubbles of reality begin to bust

We are alone

But together we trust

Wounded

My mind in distress devoid of rest

Even though i tried my best

It bounces back and makes a mess

I am broken with no emotions left

It takes its toll

You can call it theft

My eyes are damaged on how i see life

Filled with nothing but pain and strife

The wounds cut deep like a serrated knife

The darkness comes to erase the light

Natures gift

Life is a feather floating adrift

Love in the moment for that is a gift

We all need someone to hold and to lift

Indulging all senses the forth and the fifth

The sun rises a kiss to the earth

From dusk to dawn a new lights birth

A shine on darkness new worlds unearthed

Natures bold statement will stand to assert

The anatomy of life and natures cry

The bones of the earth

The eye in the sky

To breath on the wind

And fires true sin

Lights up the world for those who have been

The beauty of the world

its elegance its grace

nostalgic closer our memories make

I remember it all

for the future is at stake

Strength

I climbed emotion and reached the peak

I overcame shadow i'm strong not weak

The road looked fogged desolate and bleak

But i found some courage to get up and seek

And when i looked back i turned head and cheek

I rose to the challenge and fought my demons

I said i could manage and started believing

I could feel my hatred my doubt and my anxiety leaving

I set and focused on goals and then started achieving

The rain

The rain pours down as the clouds go dark

The clouds start to rumble and produce a spark

The lightning strikes and leaves its mark

People run and the scared dogs bark

I look out the window and begin to sigh

But then i remember this is life

The rain bring dark but also new life

And nourishes the ground so that life can thrive

It's a flourishing cycle like a bee to a hive

Spring

The sky is clearing the gardens blooming

The world spins on and keeps on moving

Flowers pop up to attract the bees

The green comes back to the bare wood trees

The wind will come and shake the leaves

I feel on my skin the clear cold breeze

I look at the sky and birds start to sing

Run my hand through grass and feel nettles sting

I stand on my feet as it begins to rain

I hold my hand with beauty comes pain

Time in nature

As time goes by i stop and stare

I smell the pine and feel the air

The trees run green and the sky runs clear

The mountains tipped the landscape bare

I close my eye and hear the noise

Insects come a kingdom will rise

They climb the trees and reach new highs

A picture perfect i say

GoodBye

My mind is a struggle

My mind is a struggle that i like to hide

Life is a journey but there is no guide

I try to take these lemons but my hands are tied

I pretend to be someone else but when alone i cried

My foundation is strong and is made of clay

But thoughts can come and ruin your day

And that's when the bricks in this building begin to sway

Then comes the collapse and it gets hard to stay

When rebuilding your life it take effort and time

And when you feel happy it feels like a crime

But when you look back and see that was your sign

It may not amount to much but at least im trying

Life is a game

I tortured myself as i lay here cold

Convinced i would die young never to see old

I felt i was drowning with no-one to hold

I struggled with this game and just wanted to fold

I pinched myself to see if its real

Because my circumstances see like a terrible deal

I wanted to return to the factory but had broken the seal

This is an issue my doctors can't heal

As i lay in bed and think about my life and my sin

As my thoughts get darker and the dark creeps in

My eyes close faster with no hope left within

My life is a game

i am never destined to win

Rise up

I could ride these storms and walk through these disasters

I will rise from these ashes and bounce back at these basterds

I could conquer this world with the confidence i've mastered

I'm not drunk on this life i'm bloody well plastered

Now i fly above these people and think that never lasted

They tried to put me down came up and got blasted

I climbed this wall and this field i've passed it

I'm high on the clouds and low in the oceans

I took what they said and put these notions into motion

I have my head on tight

I can withstand this explosion

My thoughts

My thoughts go wild and often run

With soulless emotion and the darkness stun

As the darkness brakes and up comes the sun

A feeling of warmth to which i am numb

Still in my mind i'm afraid of rejection

When life kicks you down there is no protection

Everyone can do right with a little correction

But how can i lead without a direction

As my head knocks harder and my neck gets tight

This is my pain my struggle my fight

If i could close my eyes to get through the night

But im afraid when i wake i wont see the light

They backed me to a corner and left me no option

We ran with this life like there was no stopping

But still at the end we leave in a coffin

My Anger

With my anger i feel like i could kill

But i must take a moment to consider what is real

Because i can't revert and stop the attack

Even if i wish i cant take it back

As i stand here debating he begins to taunt

I could take his life but is that what i want

I try to think differently but these feeling they haunt

I try to switch page but can't change the font

My love

Someone to love i've yet to find

But i know she is warm funny and kind

And the feeling you get will blow your mind

A deal with cupid yet to be signed

When i laugh she laughs when i cry she cries

And emotion bursts when we lock eyes

And spirits lift up as the sun will rise

She will cut your restraints to reach new highs

When i'm up or down she is there by my side

And cradle me when i just want to hide

You make me better than if i tried

And when we touch lip the angels had cried

When she stands there it's something to admire

She is my passion my goal my desire

She stands there tall like the dublin spire

Her Passion burns deep like a raging fire

I need

I need to be strong for the people i care about

I need to avoid this road and take a new route

I have old emotion i need a clear out

I'm done with the old me i ran into a tear-drought

I cared for people who wouldn't give back

I wait for a text but my screen goes black

They scavenge from people just like a rat

If it a broken record i need a new track

They cant commit

So they"re hypocrite

And i have to admit

I'm sick of it

I baby sit

For their counterfeit

And when you say something they throw a fit

I need to let go if it

Happy birthday ma

Happy birthday as we pass through time

A mother of three but always mine

Your memory is compassion reliability and kind

You help me control and improve my mind

And for that i am grateful forever in time

You are the one we fly to for guidance

Support advice were always behind you

And no matter the task we will always fight through

So until the end of time i am always beside you

Dovahkiin

From a knight's blade to an archers bow

From a blacksmiths anvil to a humble abode

A place of revels where mead barrels roll

Good tasting food to a good bards flow

A winterry tundra where tall trees grow

I am dovahkiin a dragonborn in training

An ancient title comes my naming

I conjure a thu'um the leave foes flaming

I am a mortal of a great dragons making

I escaped helgen and alduin himself

And have come here to riverwood to sell my pelt

To afford new armor and legwear with belts

To take on the world i am sure of that myself

Ingram Content Group UK Ltd.
Milton Keynes UK
UKHW020758280423
420934UK00016B/565